HEALTHY
VEGETARIAN FOOD

Food & Styling DONNA HAY
Photography QUENTIN BACON

A J.B. Fairfax Press Publication

INTRODUCTION

Vegetarian eating is a healthy alternative for today's lifestyle. Meals without meat, poultry or seafood are attractive, tasty and satisfying – as well as being good for you.

The recipes in this book provide delectable dishes which can be combined, or can be enjoyed as a hearty meal on their own. Influenced by cuisines from around the world, there are easy-to-prepare dishes which have the wonderful texture and flavour of fresh vegetables, raw and cooked.

From an Oriental-influenced soup to scrumptious desserts, this selection of satisfying and delicious recipes will enable you to prepare natural healthy food to suit every appetite and for every occasion, from a quick snack to a three-course dinner party.

UK COOKERY EDITOR
Katie Swallow

EDITORIAL
Food Editor: Rachel Blackmore
Editorial and Production Assistant: Sheridan Packer
Editorial Coordinator: Margaret Kelly

Photography: Quentin Bacon

Food and Styling: Donna Hay
Food Stylist's Assistant: Beth Pitman

DESIGN AND PRODUCTION
Manager: Sheridan Carter
Layout and Design: Lulu Dougherty
Cover Design: Frank Pithers

Published by J.B. Fairfax Press Pty Limited
80-82 McLachlan Avenue
Rushcutters Bay 2011
A.C.N. 003 738 430

Formatted by J.B. Fairfax Press Pty Limited
Printed by Toppan Printing Co, Hong Kong

© J.B. Fairfax Press Pty Limited, 1993
This book is copyright. No part may be reproduced or transmitted without the written permission of the publisher. Enquiries should be made in writing to the publisher.

JBFP 300 UK
Includes Index
ISBN 1 86343 139 X

Distributed by J. B. Fairfax Press Ltd
9 Trinity Centre, Park Farm Estate
Wellingborough, Northants
Ph: (0933) 402330 Fax: (0933) 402234

THE PANTRY SHELF

Unless otherwise stated, the following ingredients used in this book are:

Cream	Double, suitable for whipping
Flour	White flour, plain or standard
Sugar	White sugar

WHAT'S IN A TABLESPOON?

AUSTRALIA
1 tablespoon = 20 mL OR 4 teaspoons

NEW ZEALAND
1 tablespoon = 15 mL OR 3 teaspoons

UNITED KINGDOM
1 tablespoon = 15 mL OR 3 teaspoons

The recipes in this book were tested in Australia where a 20 mL tablespoon is standard. All measures are level.

The tablespoon in the New Zealand and United Kingdom sets of measuring spoons is 15 mL. For recipes using baking powder, gelatine, bicarbonate of soda, small quantities of flour and cornflour, simply add another teaspoon for each tablespoon specified.

CANNED FOOD

Can sizes vary between countries and manufacturers. You may find the quantities in this book are slightly different from what is available. Purchase and use the can size nearest to the suggested size in the recipe.

MICROWAVE IT

Where microwave instructions occur in this book a microwave oven with a 650 watt output has been used. Wattage on domestic microwave ovens varies between 500 and 700 watts, so it may be necessary to vary cooking times slightly depending on the wattage of your oven.

CONTENTS

Soups to Satisfy
4

Salads that
Make a Meal
10

Fast Food
18

Main Meals
30

Packed Lunches
44

Outdoor Feasts
50

Special Treats
58

Dreamy Desserts
64

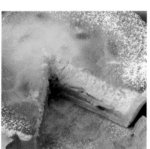

Breads and
Spreads
72

Menu Ideas
77

Index
79

SOUPS TO SATISFY

Vegetable soups can be an exciting start to a meal, or a nutritious one-bowl meal in themselves. Always ladle soup into warm bowls and serve immediately. Soups are delicious served with fresh bread or wholemeal rolls.

CELERY AND BLUE CHEESE SOUP

30 g/1 oz butter
1 bunch celery, finely chopped
2 onions, chopped
2 tablespoons flour
5 cups/1.2 litres/2 pt vegetable stock
75 g/2^1/$_2$ oz strong creamy blue cheese, mashed
freshly ground black pepper
2 tablespoons snipped fresh chives

1   Melt butter in a large saucepan. Add celery and onions and cook over a medium heat, stirring occasionally, for 4 minutes or until onions are soft but not browned.

2   Stir in flour and cook for 1 minute longer. Gradually stir in stock and mix until smooth. Bring to the boil, then reduce heat and simmer for 30 minutes, or until celery is very soft.

3   Stir in cheese and season to taste with black pepper. Ladle soup into warm bowls, sprinkle with chives and serve immediately.

Serves 6

There are several creamy blue cheeses available. Castello, Roquefort, Gorgonzola or a creamy Stilton are all suitable to use for this recipe.

Celery and Blue Cheese Soup,
Ripe Red Tomato Soup (page 6)

RIPE RED TOMATO SOUP

1 tablespoon vegetable oil
2 cloves garlic, crushed
2 fresh red chillies, finely chopped
2 red onions, chopped
4 spring onions, chopped
2 tablespoons chopped fresh thyme
or 1 teaspoon dried thyme
60 g/2 oz sun-dried tomatoes, chopped
1 kg/2 lb very ripe tomatoes,
peeled and chopped
1 cup/250 mL/8 fl oz dry white wine
4 cups/1 litre/1^3/4 pt vegetable stock
2 teaspoons sugar
^{1}/4 cup/60 g/2 oz sour cream
2 tablespoons chopped fresh basil

1   Heat oil in a large saucepan. Add garlic, chillies and red onions and cook over a medium heat, stirring, for 4 minutes or until onions are golden.

2   Add spring onions, thyme, sun-dried tomatoes, tomatoes, wine and stock. Bring to the boil, then reduce heat and simmer, covered, for 45 minutes.

3   Remove pan from heat and set aside to cool slightly. Place soup mixture, in batches, in a food processor or blender and process until smooth.

4   Return soup to a clean saucepan, add sugar, and cook over a medium heat, stirring, until hot. Serve soup topped with sour cream and basil.

Serves 6

Always a favourite, serve this refreshingly different tomato soup with Cheese and Basil Bread (page 75) or Vegetable Herb Bread (page 72).

CREAM OF LENTIL SOUP

2 teaspoons vegetable oil
1 onion, chopped
2 leeks, chopped
2 cloves garlic, crushed
315 g/10 oz green lentils
6 cups/1.5 litres/2^1/2 pt vegetable stock
or water
12 rocket leaves, roughly chopped
1 tablespoon lemon juice
^{1}/2 cup/125 mL/4 fl oz cream (single) or
^{1}/2 cup/100 g/3^1/2 oz natural yogurt

1   Heat oil in a large saucepan. Add onion, leeks and garlic and cook over a medium heat, stirring constantly, for 5 minutes or until onions are golden.

2   Stir in lentils and stock or water and bring to the boil. Reduce heat and simmer for 30 minutes or until lentils are tender. Add rocket and lemon juice and simmer for 5 minutes longer. Remove pan from heat and set aside to cool slightly.

3   Place lentil mixture, in batches, in a food processor or blender and process until smooth.

4   Return soup to a clean saucepan, bring to the boil and simmer over a medium heat for 2-3 minutes or until soup is hot. Stir in cream or yogurt.

Rocket is an old-fashioned salad herb, with a peppery taste, which is enjoying a revival. If it is unavailable, use watercress instead.
If the soup is very thick add a little extra stock or water.

Serves 6

SNOW PEA SOUP

15 g/¹/₂ oz butter
2 leeks, chopped
1 clove garlic, crushed
6 cups/1.5 litres/2¹/₂ pt vegetable stock
or water
375 g/12 oz snow peas (mangetout),
trimmed and halved
³/₄ cup/185 mL/6 fl oz cream (single)
or milk
1 tablespoon chopped fresh mint
freshly ground black pepper

CHEESE TOASTS
1 small French stick, cut into slices
100 g/3¹/₂ oz cream cheese
45 g/1¹/₂ oz grated Parmesan cheese
45 g/1¹/₂ oz grated Swiss cheese
1 teaspoon crushed black peppercorns

1   Melt butter in a large saucepan. Add leeks and garlic and cook over a medium heat, stirring, for 4 minutes or until leeks are soft.

2   Stir in stock or water and snow peas (mangetout), bring to simmering and simmer for 20 minutes. Remove pan from heat and set aside to cool slightly. Place soup mixture, in batches, in a food processor or blender and process until smooth. Push mixture through a sieve.

3   Return purée to a clean saucepan, stir in cream or milk, mint and black pepper to taste. Bring to simmering and simmer for 2 minutes or until soup is hot.

4   To make Cheese Toasts, toast bread slices under a preheated medium grill until golden on one side. Place cream cheese, Parmesan cheese, Swiss cheese and black peppercorns in a bowl and mix to combine. Spread cheese mixture over untoasted side of bread and cook under grill until cheese melts. Serve with hot soup.

Serves 6

Cheese Toasts are delicious served with other soups such as Ripe Red Tomato Soup and Cream of Lenti Soup.

---

*Cream of Lentil Soup,
Snow Pea Soup*

Plate and Terrine Accoutrement

ORIENTAL NOODLE SOUP

4 cups/1 litre/1^3/4 pt vegetable stock
^{1}/2 cup/125 mL/4 fl oz tamari
250 g/8 oz bean thread noodles
375 g/12 oz tofu, roughly chopped
155 g/5 oz bok choy, chopped
1 stalk fresh lemon grass, chopped, or
1 teaspoon dried lemon grass or
1 teaspoon finely grated lemon rind
3 spring onions, sliced diagonally
5 cm/2 in piece fresh ginger, sliced
200 g/6^1/2 oz straw or
button mushrooms
1 tablespoon chopped fresh mint
2 tablespoons chopped fresh coriander
100 g/3^1/2 oz bean sprouts

Tamari is also called *tamari shoyu* or Japanese soy sauce. Made only from natural products, soya beans and salt, it contains no MSG (monosodium glutamate) which is often found in Chinese soy sauce. It is also lighter in flavour.

1   Place stock and tamari in a large saucepan and bring to the boil. Reduce heat, add noodles, tofu, bok choy, lemon grass or lemon rind, spring onions, ginger, mushrooms, mint and coriander and simmer for 20 minutes.

2   To serve, divide bean sprouts between four warmed serving bowls and ladle over hot soup.

Serves 4

CARROT AND ORANGE SOUP

1 tablespoon vegetable oil
2 leeks, thinly sliced
6 large carrots, sliced
2 tablespoons curry powder
1 tablespoon finely grated lemon rind
1 cup/250 mL/8 fl oz orange juice
1^1/2 cups/375 mL/12 fl oz coconut milk
2 cups/500 mL/16 fl oz vegetable stock
freshly ground black pepper
^{1}/3 cup/60 g/2 oz natural yogurt
100 g/3^1/2 oz cashew nuts, roasted
and chopped
1 tablespoon chopped fresh mint

If commercially made coconut milk is unavailable, you can make it using desiccated coconut and water. To make coconut milk, place 500 g/1 lb desiccated coconut in a bowl and pour over 3 cups/ 750 mL/1^1/4 pt of boiling water. Leave to stand for 30 minutes, then strain, squeezing the coconut to extract as much liquid as possible. This will make a thick coconut milk. The coconut can be used again to make a weaker coconut milk.

1   Heat oil in a large saucepan. Add leeks and cook over a medium heat, stirring, for 5 minutes or until golden.

2   Add carrots, curry powder, lemon rind and orange juice to pan, bring to the boil and simmer for 10 minutes or until carrots are soft.

3   Stir in coconut milk and stock and simmer for 10 minutes longer.

4   Remove pan from heat and set aside to cool slightly. Place soup mixture, in batches, in a food processor or blender and process until smooth.

5   Return soup to a clean saucepan and heat over a medium heat, stirring, for 4-5 minutes or until hot. Season to taste with black pepper. Serve soup topped with yogurt, cashew nuts and mint.

Serves 4

Oriental Noodle Soup, Carrot and Orange Soup

White bowls Pillivuyt from A

SALADS THAT MAKE A MEAL

Salads have no special season. Quick to prepare, they make a wonderful accompaniment to a meal, a perfect first course or can be a complete meal in themselves at any time of the year.

MEDITERRANEAN ROCKET SALAD

100 g/3$^1/_2$ oz rocket
1 bunch curly endive, leaves separated
1 red onion, thinly sliced
440 g/14 oz canned chickpeas, drained
4 plum (egg or Italian) tomatoes, quartered
125 g/4 oz feta cheese, roughly chopped
250 g/8 oz black olives
8 marinated artichoke hearts, halved
4 tablespoons pine nuts, toasted
balsamic or red wine vinegar
freshly ground black pepper

1   Arrange rocket, endive, onion, chickpeas, tomatoes, feta cheese, olives, artichokes and pine nuts on a large serving platter.

2   Drizzle balsamic or red wine vinegar over salad and season with black pepper. Cover and chill salad until required.

Serves 4

If canned chickpeas are unavailable, use cold cooked chickpeas instead (see hint on page 16).

Mediterranean Rocket Salad, Watercress and Orange Salad (page 12)

Plates, Robyn Donoghue

WATERCRESS AND ORANGE SALAD

1 cup/185 g/6 oz burghul
(cracked wheat)
2 cups/500 mL/16 fl oz boiling water
1 bunch/250 g/8 oz watercress,
broken into sprigs
1 avocado, stoned, peeled and chopped
2 oranges, white pith removed,
flesh chopped
250 g/8 oz cherry tomatoes, halved
1 red pepper, diced

ORANGE DRESSING
$^1/_2$ cup/125 mL/4 fl oz orange juice
1 tablespoon poppy seeds
2 tablespoons red wine vinegar

1   Place burghul (cracked wheat) in a bowl, cover with boiling water and allow to stand for 10-15 minutes or until soft. Drain.

2   Place burghul (cracked wheat), watercress, avocado, oranges, tomatoes and red pepper in a salad bowl.

3   To make dressing, place orange juice, poppy seeds and vinegar in a screwtop jar and shake well to combine. Spoon dressing over salad and toss to combine. Cover and chill until required.

Serves 4

Plate Punch Gallery

Plate Accoutrement

Nashi and Nut Salad

300 g/9¹/₂ oz assorted lettuce leaves
2 nashi pears, cored and sliced
2 peaches, sliced
125 g/4 oz macadamia or brazil nuts
2 tablespoons sesame seeds, toasted

CHILLI SESAME DRESSING
2 teaspoons sesame oil
1 tablespoon vegetable oil
1 tablespoon sweet chilli sauce
2 tablespoons lemon juice

1   Arrange lettuce leaves, nashi pears, peaches, macadamia or brazil nuts and sesame seeds on a large serving platter.

2   To make dressing, place sesame and vegetable oils, chilli sauce and lemon juice in a screwtop jar and shake well to combine. Spoon dressing over salad and toss to combine. Cover and chill salad until required.

Serves 4

Native to Australia, the macadamia nut has a very hard shell and a delicious rich buttery flavour. In most recipes that call for macadamia nuts, brazil nuts can be used instead. The nashi pear is also known as the Chinese pear and is originally from northern Asia. If nashis are unavailable, pears or apples are a delicious alternative for this salad.

Left: Lentil and Mushroom Salad (page 14)
Above: Nashi and Nut Salad

LENTIL AND MUSHROOM SALAD

375 g/12 oz red lentils
250 g/8 oz button mushrooms, halved
4 spring onions, sliced diagonally
4 tablespoons pumpkin seeds
250 g/8 oz grapes
1 yellow or red pepper, chopped
4 spinach leaves, shredded

HONEY DRESSING
2 cloves garlic, crushed
1 tablespoon honey
2 tablespoons soy sauce
3 tablespoons tarragon vinegar
2 tablespoons vegetable oil
^{1}/3 cup/90 mL/3 fl oz grape juice

1   Bring a large saucepan of water to the boil. Add lentils, reduce heat and simmer for 30 minutes or until lentils are soft. Drain, rinse under cold running water and drain again.

2   Place lentils, mushrooms, spring onions, pumpkin seeds, grapes, yellow or red pepper and spinach leaves in a large bowl. Toss to combine.

3   To make dressing, place garlic, honey, soy sauce, vinegar, oil and grape juice in a screwtop jar and shake well to combine.

4   Spoon dressing over salad, cover and marinate at room temperature for 3 hours.

Serves 4-6

For a complete meal serve this salad with Vegetable Herb Bread (page 72).

ENDIVE AND GOAT'S CHEESE SALAD

8 thick slices goat's cheese
1 tablespoon olive oil
freshly ground black pepper
300 g/9^1/2 oz curly endive leaves
250 g/8 oz cherry tomatoes, halved
1 cucumber, sliced
1 small French stick, sliced and toasted
2 tablespoons white wine vinegar

1   Brush goat's cheese with oil and season with black pepper. Place under a preheated medium grill and cook for 3 minutes each side or until golden.

2   Arrange endive leaves, tomatoes, cucumber, toast and goat's cheese on a serving platter. Drizzle with vinegar and serve immediately.

Serves 4

A simple yet delicious salad with a strong Mediterranean influence. Curly endive is a member of the chicory family and has a more bitter taste than lettuce.

*Chickpea and Pepper Salad (page 16),
Endive and Goat's Cheese Salad*

Plates Robyn Donoghue

CHICKPEA AND PEPPER SALAD

If yellow peppers are unavailable, use another red pepper.
If canned chickpeas are unavailable, use cold cooked chickpeas instead. To cook chickpeas, soak overnight in cold water. Drain. Place in a large saucepan, cover with cold water and bring to the boil over a medium heat. Reduce heat and simmer for 45-60 minutes or until chickpeas are tender. Drain and cool.

2 teaspoons vegetable oil
1 red pepper, roughly chopped
1 green pepper, roughly chopped
1 yellow pepper, roughly chopped
2 cloves garlic, crushed
4 spring onions, sliced diagonally
2 x 440 g/14 oz canned chickpeas, drained
4 tablespoons pine nuts, toasted

PINE NUT DRESSING
4 tablespoons pine nuts, toasted
2 tablespoons olive oil
2 tablespoons lemon juice
3 tablespoons vegetable stock or water
1 tablespoon chopped fresh coriander

Serves 6

1   Heat oil in a large frying pan. Add red, green and yellow peppers, garlic and spring onions and cook over a medium heat, stirring constantly, for 5 minutes or until peppers are soft. Remove pan from heat and set aside to cool.

2   Place chickpeas, pine nuts and pepper mixture in a salad bowl and toss to combine.

3   To make dressing, place pine nuts, oil, lemon juice, stock or water and coriander in a food processor or blender and process until smooth. Spoon dressing over salad, toss to combine, cover and chill until ready to serve.

BLACK-EYED BEAN SALAD

Choose assorted lettuce leaves from among the following varieties: cos, butter (round), oakleaf, mignonette (lollo rosso) and iceberg. Many supermarkets and greengrocers now offer salad mix (a mixture of salad greens) which is ideal for this recipe and for those calling for assorted lettuce leaves.

250 g/8 oz black-eyed beans
2 tablespoons balsamic or red wine vinegar
1 red onion, finely chopped
3 ripe tomatoes, chopped
2 tablespoons chopped fresh basil
1 tablespoon chopped fresh mint
1 eggplant (aubergine), sliced
2 tablespoons olive oil
200 g/6^{1}/2 oz assorted lettuce leaves

Serves 4

1   Place beans in a large bowl, cover with water and set aside to soak overnight, then drain. Bring a large saucepan of water to the boil, add beans and boil for 10 minutes. Reduce heat and cook for 20-30 minutes or until beans are soft. Drain and set aside to cool.

2   Place beans, vinegar, onion, tomatoes, basil and mint in a bowl, toss to combine and set aside for 20 minutes.

3   Brush eggplant (aubergine) slices lightly with oil. Place under a preheated hot grill and cook for 2 minutes each side or until golden.

4   Arrange lettuce leaves, bean mixture and eggplant (aubergine) on a serving platter. Serve at room temperature.

Italian Salad, Black-eyed Bean Salad

ITALIAN SALAD

300 g/9¹/₂ oz assorted lettuce leaves
12 sun-dried tomatoes, chopped
60 g/2 oz sun-dried peppers, chopped
8 canned artichoke hearts, halved
125 g/4 oz black olives
6 bocconcini cheeses or 250 g/8 oz
mozzarella cheese, sliced
2 tablespoons chopped fresh basil

PESTO DRESSING
4 tablespoons ready-made pesto
¹/₂ cup/125 mL/4 fl oz mayonnaise or
¹/₂ cup/100 g/3¹/₂ oz natural yogurt

1   Arrange lettuce leaves, sun-dried tomatoes, sun-dried peppers, artichokes, olives and cheese in a salad bowl. Sprinkle with basil.

2   To make dressing, place pesto and mayonnaise or yogurt in a bowl and mix to combine. Spoon dressing over salad, cover and chill until required.

Serves 4

If sun-dried peppers are unavailable, use roasted peppers or bottled peppers in olive oil marinade.

Basket Accoutrement

FAST FOOD

*If you have little time for preparation and cooking,
yet you want your meals to be interesting and delicious, the
dishes in this chapter will be perfect for you.*

GOAT'S CHEESE AND POLENTA PIZZA

CORN MEAL (POLENTA) BASE
100 g/3$^{1}/_{2}$ oz self-raising flour
155 g/5 oz corn meal (polenta)
2 eggs, lightly beaten
$^{3}/_{4}$ cup/185 mL/6 fl oz milk
1 tablespoon olive oil

RED PEPPER TOPPING
3 tablespoons tomato paste (purée)
2 red peppers, roasted and skins
removed
125 g/4 oz button mushrooms, sliced
125 g/4 oz marinated eggplant
(aubergines)
125 g/4 oz goat's cheese, crumbled or
chopped
1 tablespoon fresh oregano or
$^{1}/_{2}$ teaspoon dried oregano
freshly ground black pepper

1 To make base, place flour and corn
meal (polenta) in a bowl. Make a well in
the centre and stir in eggs and milk to
form a smooth batter.

2 Heat oil in a 25 cm/10 in heavy-based
frying pan over a medium heat. Pour in
batter and cook for 5 minutes. Carefully
turn base over in pan and cook for 5
minutes longer. Remove pan from heat.

3 For topping, spread base with tomato
paste (purée) and top with red peppers,
mushrooms, eggplant (aubergines), goat's
cheese, oregano and black pepper to
taste.

4 Place pizza in pan under a preheated
hot grill and cook for 3 minutes or until
topping is hot. Serve hot or cold, cut into
wedges.

Serves 4

Marinated eggplant
(aubergines) are available
from Italian delicatessens
and the delicatessen section
of some supermarkets.

*Watercress and Stilton Pizzas (page 20),
Goat's Cheese and Polenta Pizza*

WATERCRESS AND STILTON PIZZAS

6 small pitta bread rounds
1 bunch/250 g/8 oz watercress, broken
into sprigs
3 pears, cored, peeled and sliced
200 g/6¹/₂ oz Stilton or other blue
cheese, sliced
freshly ground black pepper

1   Toast pitta bread rounds under a
preheated medium grill for 2-3 minutes
each side or until crisp.

2   Top each pitta bread round with
watercress, pears, cheese and black pepper
to taste.

3   Return to grill and cook for 1 minute
or until cheese melts and pears are warm.

Serves 6

These pizzas are delicious
served with Lentil and
Mushroom Salad (page 14).
Leftover pizzas are a tasty
addition to a packed lunch.

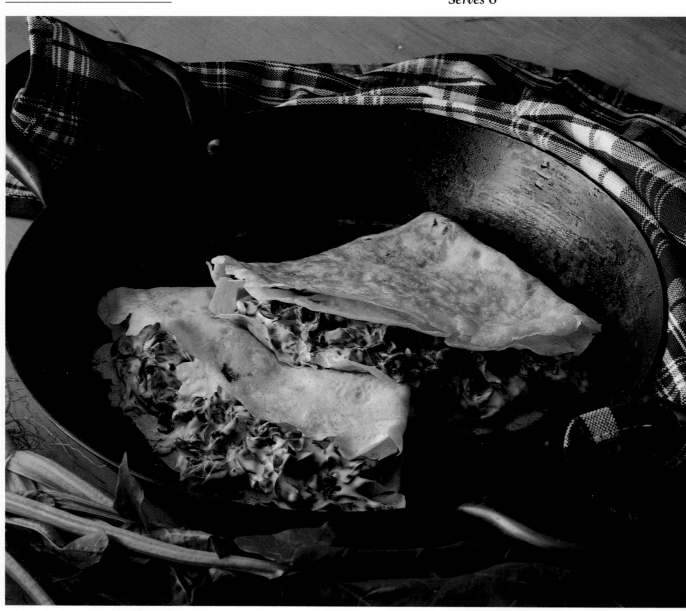

Plate Accoutrement

SPICY BUCKWHEAT NOODLES

500 g/1 lb buckwheat noodles
1 tablespoon olive oil
3 cloves garlic, crushed
2 fresh red chillies, seeded and chopped
200 g/6^1/$_2$ oz rocket leaves
removed and shredded
2 tomatoes, chopped

1   Cook noodles in boiling water in a large saucepan following packet directions. Drain, set aside and keep warm.

2   Heat oil in a frying pan. Add garlic and cook over a medium heat, stirring, for 1 minute. Add chillies, rocket and tomatoes and cook for 2 minutes longer or until rocket wilts. Toss vegetable mixture with noodles and serve immediately.

Left: Spinach Pancakes (page 22)
Above: Spicy Buckwheat Noodles

Serves 4

If rocket is unavailable you can use watercress instead. For a complete meal, accompany with a tossed green salad and wholemeal bread rolls.

SPINACH PANCAKES

Oven temperature
180°C, 350°F, Gas 4

SPINACH PANCAKES
8 spinach or silverbeet leaves, shredded
1 cup/125 g/4 oz flour
4 eggs, lightly beaten
155 mL/5 fl oz milk
30 g/1 oz butter, melted

SPINACH FILLING
2 teaspoons vegetable oil
2 cloves garlic, crushed
12 spinach or silverbeet leaves, shredded
300 g/9¹/₂ oz sour cream or
natural yogurt
freshly ground black pepper

1   To make pancakes, boil or microwave spinach or silverbeet until wilted. Drain and squeeze out as much liquid as possible.

2   Place flour in a bowl and make a well in the centre. Add eggs and a little milk and beat, working in all the flour. Beat in butter and remaining milk, then stir through spinach.

3   Pour 2-3 tablespoons of batter into a 20 cm/8 in nonstick frying pan and tilt pan so batter evenly covers base. Cook for 1 minute each side or until lightly browned. Set aside and keep warm. Repeat with remaining batter.

4   To make filling, heat oil in a frying pan, add garlic and cook over a medium heat, stirring, for 1 minute. Add spinach or silverbeet and cook for 3 minutes longer or until spinach or silverbeet wilts.

5   Stir in sour cream or yogurt and black pepper to taste. Spread a spoonful of filling over each pancake. Fold pancakes into quarters and serve immediately.

Serves 6

These wholesome pancakes envelop a delicious savoury filling and are best served immediately after cooking. For a complete meal, serve with a tossed green salad.

GREEN OMELETTE

15 g/¹/₂ oz butter
8 sorrel leaves, shredded
1 teaspoon green peppercorns in
brine, drained
2 tablespoons dry white wine
4 eggs, lightly beaten
1 cup/250 mL/8 fl oz milk

1   Melt butter in a large frying pan. Add sorrel and cook over a medium heat, stirring, for 1 minute or until sorrel wilts. Add green peppercorns and wine and cook, stirring, for 1 minute longer.

2   Place eggs and milk in a bowl and whisk to combine.

3   Pour egg mixture into frying pan and cook over a low heat for 4-5 minutes or until egg mixture is set. Place pan under a preheated hot grill and cook until top of omelette is golden. Serve cut into wedges.

Serves 3

Sorrel is another old-fashioned herb that is enjoying a revival. It was used by the Romans and has long been popular in European countries. It has a lemony flavour and is easy to grow. If sorrel is unavailable, use English spinach instead.

HERB AND POTATO TORTILLA

1 tablespoon vegetable oil
3 potatoes, chopped
2 onions, chopped
6 eggs, lightly beaten
$^1/_2$ cup/125 mL/4 fl oz milk
125 g/4 oz blue cheese, crumbled
2 tablespoons chopped fresh parsley
freshly ground black pepper
8 small fresh basil leaves
8 fresh oregano leaves

1   Heat oil in a large frying pan. Add potatoes and onions and cook over a low heat for 8-10 minutes or until potatoes are tender.

2   Place eggs, milk, blue cheese, parsley and black pepper to taste in a bowl and whisk to combine.

3   Pour egg mixture over potato mixture in the pan and top with basil and oregano leaves. Cook over a low heat for 6 minutes or until egg mixture is set.

4   Place pan under a preheated hot grill and cook until top of tortilla is golden. Serve hot or cold, cut into wedges.

Herb and Potato Tortilla,
Green Omelette

Serves 4

If fresh basil and oregano are unavailable use dried instead. Add $^1/_2$ teaspoon of each to the potato mixture.

23

PASTA WITH CHICKPEAS AND FETA

Include basil, tarragon and parsley in your fresh mixed herbs. Serve this dish warm or cold as a pasta salad. Cold cooked chickpeas can be used instead of canned chickpeas (see hint on page 16).

500 g/1 lb dried ribbon pasta

CHICKPEA AND FETA SAUCE
2 x 440 g/14 oz canned
chickpeas, drained
6 tomatoes, chopped
300 g/9^1/$_2$ oz feta cheese,
roughly chopped
^{1}/$_3$ cup/90 mL/3 fl oz balsamic vinegar
3 tablespoons chopped fresh mixed herbs
8 sun-dried tomatoes, chopped
1 tablespoon capers, drained (optional)

1   Cook pasta in boiling water in a large saucepan following packet directions. Drain, set aside and keep warm.

2   Place chickpeas, tomatoes, cheese, vinegar, herbs, sun-dried tomatoes and capers in a bowl and mix to combine. Toss chickpea mixture with warm pasta.

Serves 6

PASTA WITH FRESH THYME

500 g/1 lb fresh herb pasta or plain pasta
freshly ground black pepper
fresh Parmesan cheese

THYME SAUCE
60 g/2 oz butter
^{1}/$_3$ cup/90 mL/3 fl oz white wine vinegar
3 tablespoons roughly chopped
fresh thyme

To make shavings of Parmesan cheese you will need a piece of fresh Parmesan cheese. Use a vegetable peeler or a coarse grater to remove shavings of cheese.

1   Cook pasta in boiling water in a large saucepan following packet directions. Drain, set aside and keep warm.

2   To make sauce, melt butter in a small saucepan and add vinegar and thyme. Bring to simmering and simmer over a low heat, stirring, for 4 minutes.

3   Spoon sauce over pasta and toss to combine. Season to taste with black pepper and top with shavings of Parmesan cheese.

Serves 4

Pasta with Fresh Thyme,
Pasta with Chickpeas and Feta

EGGPLANT KEBABS

2 cloves garlic, crushed
1 tablespoon vegetable oil
2 teaspoons ground cumin
8 baby eggplant (aubergines), sliced in
half lengthwise

YOGURT SAUCE
3/4 cup/155 g/5 oz natural yogurt
2 tablespoons chopped fresh coriander
2 tablespoons chopped fresh mint

1   Place garlic, oil and cumin in a small bowl and whisk to combine. Brush oil mixture over cut sides of eggplant (aubergines).

2   Thread eggplant (aubergines) onto lightly oiled skewers and cook on a hot grill or under a preheated hot grill for 4 minutes each side or until tender.

3   To make sauce, place yogurt, coriander and mint in a small bowl and mix to combine. Serve sauce with hot kebabs.

Serves 4

For a complete meal, accompany this dish with pitta bread and a salad.

SPINACH RICE PARCELS

8 spinach leaves, stalks removed
1 cup/250 mL/8 fl oz vegetable stock

RICE FILLING
1 cup/220 g/7 oz rice, cooked
1 cup/220 g/7 oz wild rice, cooked
2 spring onions, chopped
1 avocado, stoned, peeled and chopped
1 tablespoon finely grated orange rind
3 tablespoons sultanas
2 tomatoes, finely chopped
freshly ground black pepper

1   Boil, steam or microwave spinach leaves until wilted. Drain and pat dry with absorbent kitchen paper.

2   To make filling, place rice, wild rice, spring onions, avocado, orange rind, sultanas, tomatoes and black pepper to taste in a bowl and mix to combine.

3   Divide rice mixture between spinach leaves. Fold in sides of leaves and roll up to form a parcel.

4   Arrange spinach parcels side by side in a shallow ovenproof dish. Pour over stock, cover and bake for 15 minutes or until heated through.

Left: Eggplant Kebabs
Below: Spinach Rice Parcels

Serves 4

Oven temperature
180°C, 350°F, Gas 4

The rice parcels can be cooked in the microwave. Place the prepared parcels in a microwave-safe dish, pour over 1/2 cup/125 mL/ 4 fl oz stock, cover and cook on HIGH (100%) for 5-8 minutes or until heated. For a complete meal serve with natural yogurt and a mixed green salad.

Mushroom Frittata

15 g/¹/₂ oz butter
500 g/1 lb mixed fresh mushrooms
3 tablespoons snipped fresh chives
1 tablespoon green peppercorns in
brine, drained
2 teaspoons finely grated lemon rind
8 eggs, lightly beaten
1 cup/200 g/6¹/₂ oz natural yogurt
2 tablespoons chopped fresh basil or
1 teaspoon dried basil
4 tablespoons grated Parmesan cheese

1 Melt butter in a large frying pan.
Add mushrooms, chives and green
peppercorns and cook over a medium
heat, stirring, for 5 minutes.

2 Place lemon rind, eggs, yogurt and
basil in a bowl and whisk to combine.

3 Pour egg mixture over mushrooms and
cook over a low heat for 6 minutes or
until just set.

4 Sprinkle with Parmesan cheese and
cook under a preheated grill for 1 minute
or until cheese melts and is golden.

Serves 4

Use whatever mushrooms
are available to make this
frittata. You might like to try
a combination of button,
shiitake and oyster
mushrooms or use just flat
mushrooms. Serve Mushroom
Frittata cut into wedges
with wholemeal toast or
crusty rolls.

EASY VEGETABLE STIR-FRY

100 g/3¹/₂ oz dried mushrooms
2 teaspoons sesame oil
2 cloves garlic, crushed
1 tablespoon grated fresh ginger
1 large onion, sliced
1 red pepper, cut into strips
2 carrots, sliced diagonally
250 g/8 oz broccoli, cut into florets
3 stalks celery, sliced diagonally
350 g/11 oz canned baby sweet
corn, drained
200 g/6¹/₂ oz firm tofu, chopped
2 tablespoons sweet chilli sauce
2 tablespoons soy sauce
4 tablespoons cashew nuts

1   Place mushrooms in a bowl and cover with boiling water. Set aside to stand for 15-20 minutes or until mushrooms are tender. Drain, remove stalks if necessary and slice mushrooms.

2   Heat oil in a wok or frying pan, add garlic, ginger and onion and stir-fry over a medium heat for 3 minutes or until onion is soft.

3   Add red pepper, carrots, broccoli and celery and stir-fry for 3 minutes longer.

4   Add mushrooms, sweet corn, tofu, chilli sauce, soy sauce and cashews and stir-fry for 1 minute longer. Serve immediately.

Left: Mushroom Frittata
Above: Easy Vegetable Stir-Fry

Serves 4

For a complete meal accompany this easy stir-fry with boiled rice or pasta. Originally a Chinese cooking method, stir-frying is now a popular way of cooking vegetables around the world. The short cooking time means that the vegetables retain their colour, texture and vitamins.

MAIN MEALS

In this chapter you will find colourful and tasty dishes, which capture the flavours of a variety of international cuisines. All the dishes are substantial and delicious enough to be main meals in their own right, perhaps accompanied by a salad or steamed vegetables, or some crusty fresh bread.

OKRA AND BEAN STEW

2 teaspoons vegetable oil
2 cloves garlic, crushed
2 fresh red chillies, chopped
2 onions, sliced
250 g/8 oz okra
2 eggplant (aubergines), chopped
2 x 440 g/14 oz canned peeled tomatoes,
undrained and mashed
440 g/14 oz canned red kidney
beans, rinsed
250 g/8 oz firm tofu, cut into chunks
$^{1}/_{2}$ cup/125 mL/4 fl oz red wine
1 tablespoon brown sugar
3 tablespoons chopped fresh basil
freshly ground black pepper

1   Heat oil in a large saucepan. Add garlic, chillies and onions and cook over a medium heat, stirring constantly, for 5 minutes or until onions are soft and golden.

2   Add okra, eggplant (aubergines), tomatoes, beans, tofu, wine and sugar. Bring to the boil, then reduce heat and simmer for 30 minutes. Stir in basil and black pepper to taste.

Serves 4

Serve this tasty vegetable stew with boiled wholemeal pasta or brown rice.
When preparing fresh okra, wash it well and handle it carefully. Rub it gently under running water to remove the outer fuzzy layer.

Okra and Bean Stew,
Ricotta and Basil Lasagne (page 32)

RICOTTA AND BASIL LASAGNE

Oven temperature
190°C, 375°F, Gas 5

4 eggplant (aubergines), sliced
salt
olive oil
1 bunch fresh basil, leaves removed
from stems
500 g/1 lb ricotta cheese, drained
300 g/9^{1}/$_{2}$ oz mozzarella cheese, sliced

TOMATO SAUCE
2 teaspoons vegetable oil
2 onions, chopped
2 cloves garlic, crushed
2 x 440 g/14 oz canned peeled tomatoes,
undrained and mashed
^{1}/$_{2}$ cup/125 mL/4 fl oz red wine
2 teaspoons sugar

1   Place eggplant (aubergine) slices in a colander set over a bowl and sprinkle with salt. Set aside to stand for 10 minutes, then rinse under cold running water and pat dry with absorbent kitchen paper.

2   Brush eggplant (aubergine) slices with

oil and cook under a preheated medium grill for 2-4 minutes each side or until golden.

3   To make sauce, heat oil in a saucepan, add onions and garlic and cook over a medium heat, stirring constantly, for 3 minutes or until onions are soft. Stir in tomatoes, wine and sugar, bring to the boil and simmer for 10 minutes or until sauce reduces and thickens.

4   Line the base of an ovenproof dish with one-third of the eggplant (aubergine) slices, top with one-third of the basil leaves, one-third of the tomato sauce, one-third of the ricotta cheese and one-third of the mozzarella cheese. Repeat layers finishing with a layer of mozzarella cheese. Bake for 30 minutes or until hot and bubbling and top is golden.

Serves 6

For a complete meal, serve this lasagne with wholegrain bread or rolls and a tossed green salad.

CHILLI PASTA BAKE

Oven temperature
180°C, 350°F, Gas 4

375 g/12 oz penne pasta
300 g/9^{1}/$_{2}$ oz sour cream
125 g/4 oz tasty cheese (mature
Cheddar), grated

CHILLI SAUCE
2 teaspoons vegetable oil
2 onions, chopped
1 teaspoon ground cumin
1 teaspoon ground coriander
^{1}/$_{2}$ teaspoon chilli powder
440 g/14 oz canned red kidney beans,
drained
440 g/14 oz canned tomato purée

1   Cook pasta in boiling water in a large saucepan following packet directions. Drain, stir in sour cream and spread over base of an ovenproof dish.

2   To make sauce, heat oil in a large saucepan. Add onions and cook over a medium heat, stirring, for 3 minutes or until onions are soft. Add cumin, coriander and chilli powder and cook, stirring constantly, for 1 minute longer. Stir in beans and tomato purée, bring to the boil and simmer for 5 minutes.

3   Pour sauce over pasta, sprinkle with cheese and bake for 15-20 minutes or until cheese melts and is golden.

Serve this tasty bake with steamed vegetables and Cheese and Basil Bread (page 75).

Serves 4

TAGLIARINI WITH PISTACHIOS

500 g/1 lb fresh spinach tagliarini
45 g/1¹/₂ oz butter
60 g/2 oz pistachio nuts, shelled
4 tablespoons shredded fresh basil leaves
250 g/8 oz cherry tomatoes, halved
1 tablespoon green peppercorns in brine, drained

1   Cook tagliarini in boiling water in a large saucepan following packet directions. Drain, set aside and keep warm.

2   Melt butter in a frying pan, add pistachio nuts, basil, tomatoes and green peppercorns. Cook over a medium heat, stirring constantly, for 4-5 minutes or until heated through. Toss tomato mixture with pasta.

Tagliarini is a flat ribbon pasta similar to tagliatelle but slightly narrower in width. If unavailable this dish is also delicious made with tagliatelle, fettuccine or spaghetti.

Tagliarini with Pistachios, Chilli Pasta Bake

Serves 4

Bowl Punch Gallery

33

ITALIAN POTATO BAKE

Oven temperature
200°C, 400°F, Gas 6

A hearty meal for a cold winter's night, it is delicious served with a tomato and onion salad or a stir-fry of mixed vegetables.

6 potatoes, sliced
$^1/_2$ cup/125 g/4 oz ready-made pesto
2 yellow or green zucchini (courgettes),
sliced lengthwise
$^1/_2$ cup/125 g/4 oz olive paste (pâté)
6 baby eggplant (aubergines),
sliced lengthwise
$^1/_2$ cup/125 mL/4 fl oz milk
$^1/_2$ cup/125 g/4 oz sour cream
60 g/2 oz grated Parmesan cheese
freshly ground black pepper

1 Arrange one-third of the potatoes over the base of a large ovenproof dish. Top with pesto, zucchini (courgettes) and half of the remaining potatoes.

2 Top potatoes with olive paste (pâté), eggplant (aubergines) and remaining potatoes.

3 Place milk and sour cream in a bowl, mix to combine and carefully pour over potatoes. Sprinkle with Parmesan cheese and black pepper to taste and bake for 50 minutes or until potatoes are tender.

Serves 4

Plate Villeroy & Boch

34

ASPARAGUS AND CHEESE TART

Left: Italian Potato Bake
Above: Asparagus and Cheese Tart

300 g/9¹/₂ oz prepared shortcrust pastry

ASPARAGUS AND SMOKED
CHEESE FILLING
**2 teaspoons vegetable oil
2 leeks, chopped
350 g/11 oz asparagus spears, trimmed
and cut in half
3 eggs, lightly beaten
³/₄ cup/185 mL/6 fl oz milk
125 g/4 oz smoked cheese, grated
freshly ground black pepper**

1   Roll out pastry to 3 mm/¹/₄ in thick and use to line a 23 cm/9 in lightly greased flan tin. Prick base and sides of pastry case with a fork, line with nonstick baking paper and fill with uncooked rice.

Bake for 10 minutes or until lightly browned. Remove rice and paper and set aside to cool.

2   To make filling, heat oil in a frying pan, add leeks and cook over a medium heat, stirring, for 4 minutes or until leeks are golden. Remove pan from heat and set aside to cool.

3   Scatter asparagus over base of pastry case. Place eggs, milk, cheese, black pepper to taste and cooked leeks in a bowl and mix to combine. Pour egg mixture over asparagus, reduce oven temperature to 180°C/350°F/Gas 4 and bake for 35-40 minutes or until filling is firm.

Serves 4-6

Oven temperature
190°C, 375°F, Gas 5

For a more substantial and impressive tart double the quantity of the filling and cook in a deep-sided flan tin. You will need to increase the cooking time by 15-20 minutes.

BAKED POLENTA SANDWICHES

Oven temperature
180°C, 350°F, Gas 4

POLENTA
1 cup/170 g/5^1/$_2$ oz corn meal (polenta)
2 cups/500 mL/16 fl oz hot
vegetable stock
75 g/2^1/$_2$ oz blue cheese, crumbled
30 g/1 oz grated Parmesan cheese

VEGETABLE FILLING
2 teaspoons vegetable oil
1 red pepper, cut into strips
1 yellow or green pepper, cut into strips
1 zucchini (courgette), cut into strips
8 sun-dried tomatoes, chopped
125 g/4 oz feta cheese, chopped
2 tablespoons balsamic or red
wine vinegar

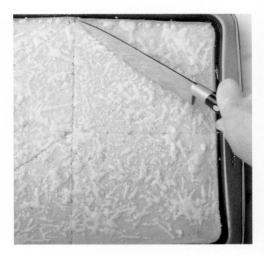

1 To make Polenta, place corn meal
(polenta) and 1 cup/250 mL/8 fl oz of
stock in a saucepan and whisk until
smooth. Place over a medium heat and
cook, gradually stirring in remaining
stock. Continue cooking, stirring
constantly, for 15-20 minutes or until
corn meal (polenta) leaves the side of
pan. Stir in blue cheese.

2 Spread corn meal (polenta) mixture
over the base of a greased 26 x 32 cm/
10^1/$_2$ x 12^3/$_4$ in Swiss roll tin, sprinkle
with Parmesan cheese and bake for 10
minutes or until firm and cheese melts
and is golden.

3 To make filling, heat oil in a frying
pan, add red pepper, yellow or green
pepper, zucchini (courgette) and sun-
dried tomatoes and cook over a high heat,
stirring constantly, for 4 minutes or until
vegetables are just soft. Stir in feta cheese
and vinegar.

4 To assemble, cut Polenta into eight
triangles. Top one triangle with one-
quarter of filling, then with a second
triangle. Repeat with remaining triangles
and filling to make four sandwiches.

Serves 4

Corn meal (polenta) is
cooked yellow maize flour
and is very popular in
northern Italian cooking.
Corn meal (polenta) refers to
both the name of a dish and
the yellow maize flour.

SUN-DRIED TOMATO GNOCCHI

4 tablespoons grated Parmesan cheese

TOMATO GNOCCHI
500 g/1 lb cooked potatoes
2 egg yolks
1 cup/125 g/4 oz flour
12 sun-dried tomatoes, chopped

OLIVE SAUCE
2 teaspoons olive oil
1 onion, chopped
2 cloves garlic, crushed
125 g/4 oz chopped black olives
2 tablespoons chopped fresh parsley
$^1/_3$ cup/90 mL/3 fl oz red wine

For a balanced meal start with a soup such as Celery and Blue Cheese Soup (page 4). Accompany the gnocchi with a salad or steamed vegetables and finish the meal with fresh fruit or a dessert such as Caramelised Rice Puddings (page 68).

1 To make gnocchi, place potatoes in a bowl and mash until smooth. Mix in egg yolks, flour and sun-dried tomatoes to form a stiff dough.

2 Shape small spoonfuls into oval shapes. Cook gnocchi in batches in boiling water in a large saucepan for 3 minutes or until they rise to the surface. Using a slotted spoon remove gnocchi from pan and place in a greased ovenproof dish. Sprinkle with Parmesan cheese and bake for 15-20 minutes or until cheese melts and is golden.

3 To make sauce, heat oil in a saucepan, add onion and garlic and cook over a medium heat, stirring, for 3 minutes or until onion is soft. Add olives, parsley and wine and cook, stirring, for 3 minutes longer. Spoon sauce over gnocchi and serve immediately.

Serves 4

Plate Villeroy & Boch

Left: Sun-dried Tomato Gnocchi
Above: Cheese and Herb Fritters

CHEESE AND HERB FRITTERS

CHEESE FRITTERS
125 g/4 oz feta cheese, crumbled
125 g/4 oz tasty cheese (mature
Cheddar), finely chopped
125 g/4 oz Swiss cheese, finely chopped
$^1/_3$ cup/45 g/1$^1/_2$ oz flour
2 eggs, lightly beaten
$^1/_4$ cup/60 mL/2 fl oz milk
3 tablespoons chopped fresh
mixed herbs

AVOCADO SALSA
1 avocado, stoned, peeled and chopped
2 tablespoons lime or lemon juice
1 fresh red chilli, chopped
1 small red onion, finely chopped

1   To make salsa, place avocado, lime or lemon juice, chilli and onion in a small bowl and mix to combine.

2   To make fritters, place feta cheese, tasty cheese (mature Cheddar), Swiss cheese, flour, eggs, milk and herbs in a bowl and mix well.

3   Cook large spoonfuls of batter in a nonstick frying pan over a medium heat for 2 minutes each side or until golden. Serve fritters immediately with salsa.

Serves 4

For a complete meal serve with Vegetable Herb Bread (page 72) and a tossed green salad.
The salsa is a spicy version of the Mexican dip, guacamole, and is also delicious served as a dip with raw or lightly steamed vegetables.

MUSHROOM RISOTTO

45 g/1¹/₂ oz butter
200 g/6¹/₂ oz flat mushrooms,
thickly sliced
125 g/4 oz button mushrooms, halved
200 g/6¹/₂ oz shiitake mushrooms
200 g/6¹/₂ oz oyster mushrooms
2 cups/440 g/14 oz Arborio or
risotto rice
4 cups/1 litre/1³/₄ pt hot vegetable stock
4 tablespoons grated Parmesan cheese
freshly ground black pepper

Arborio or risotto rice is
traditionally used for making
risottos. It absorbs liquid
without becoming soft and it
is this special quality that
makes it so suitable for
risottos. If Arborio rice is
unavailable, substitute short
grain rice. A risotto made in
the traditional way, where
liquid is added a little at a
time as the rice cooks, will
take 20-30 minutes to cook.

1 Melt 15 g/¹/₂ oz butter in a frying pan.
Add flat, button, shiitake and oyster
mushrooms and cook over a medium
heat, stirring constantly, for 4-5 minutes
or until mushrooms are soft. Remove pan
from heat and set aside.

2 Melt remaining butter in a clean
frying pan. Add rice and cook over a
medium heat, stirring constantly, for 2
minutes. Pour 1 cup/250 mL/8 fl oz hot
stock into rice and cook over a medium
heat, stirring constantly, until stock is
absorbed. Continue cooking in this way
until all the stock is used and rice is just
tender.

3 Stir mushroom mixture, Parmesan
cheese and black pepper to taste into rice
mixture and cook for 2 minutes longer.

Serves 4

TOMATO RISOTTO

4 cups/1 litre/1³/₄ pt vegetable stock
2 cups/500 mL/16 fl oz tomato juice
15 g/¹/₂ oz butter
2³/₄ cups/600 g/1¹/₄ lb Arborio or
risotto rice
10 sun-dried tomatoes, sliced
2 tomatoes, chopped
125 g/4 oz pitted olives
freshly ground black pepper

When serving a risotto, start
with a salad and crusty
bread and finish with fresh
fruit or a dessert such as
Baked Mandarin Sabayon
(page 66).

1 Place stock and tomato juice in a large
saucepan and bring to the boil over a
medium heat. Reduce heat and keep
warm.

2 Melt butter in a large saucepan. Add
rice and cook over a medium heat,
stirring constantly, for 3 minutes. Pour
1 cup/250 mL/8 fl oz stock mixture into
rice and cook over a medium heat,
stirring constantly, until stock is absorbed.
Continue cooking in this way until all
the stock is used and rice is tender.

3 Stir sun-dried tomatoes, tomatoes,
olives and black pepper to taste into rice
mixture and cook for 2 minutes longer.

Serves 6

Mushroom Risotto, Tomato Risotto

VEGETABLE CURRY WITH CHUTNEY

VEGETABLE CURRY
2 teaspoons vegetable oil
1 teaspoon ground cumin
1 tablespoon curry paste
2 onions, chopped
2 potatoes, finely chopped
200 g/6^1/$_2$ oz cauliflower, cut into florets
200 g/6^1/$_2$ oz broccoli, cut into florets
155 g/5 oz green beans, halved
1 red pepper, chopped
2 zucchini (courgettes), chopped
200 mL/6^1/$_2$ fl oz coconut milk
200 mL/6^1/$_2$ fl oz vegetable stock

RHUBARB CHUTNEY
500 g/1 lb rhubarb, chopped
1 tablespoon grated fresh ginger
1 fresh green chilli, chopped
1 tablespoon black mustard seeds
^{3}/$_4$ cup/125 g/4 oz brown sugar
1 cup/250 mL/8 fl oz white vinegar
60 g/2 oz currants

Serve this curry with jasmine or basmati rice.
Rhubarb Chutney can be stored in sterilised airtight jars for several months.

1 To make chutney, place rhubarb, ginger, chilli, mustard seeds, sugar, vinegar and currants in a saucepan and cook over a medium heat, stirring occasionally, for 30 minutes or until mixture is soft and pulpy.

2 To make curry, heat oil in a large saucepan, add cumin, curry paste and onions and cook, stirring, for 3 minutes or until onions are soft. Add potatoes, cauliflower, broccoli, beans, red pepper, zucchini (courgettes), coconut milk and stock and bring to the boil. Reduce heat and simmer, stirring occasionally, for 25-35 minutes or until vegetables are tender. Serve curry with Rhubarb Chutney.

Serves 4

Plate and Bowl Villeroy & Boch

42

VEGETABLES WITH SAFFRON CREAM

Left: Vegetable Curry with Chutney
Above: Vegetables with Saffron Cream

4 large potatoes, quartered
8 slices pumpkin or 4 carrots,
halved lengthwise
4 onions, halved
4 parsnips, halved
4 zucchini (courgettes), halved
lengthwise

SAFFRON CREAM
300 g/9$^{1}/_{2}$ oz sour cream
2 bay leaves
pinch saffron threads
$^{1}/_{2}$ teaspoon coriander seeds
$^{1}/_{2}$ teaspoon cumin seeds

1   Place potatoes, pumpkin or carrots,
onions, parsnips and zucchini (courgettes)
in a well-greased baking dish and bake,
turning occasionally, for 40-45 minutes or
until vegetables are tender.

2   To make Saffron Cream, place sour
cream, bay leaves, saffron threads,
coriander seeds and cumin seeds in a small
saucepan and cook over a low heat,
stirring constantly, for 3 minutes. Push
mixture through a sieve and serve with
roast vegetables.

Serves 4

Oven temperature
200°C, 400°F, Gas 6

When serving this dish you
might like to serve a soup
such as Cream of Lentil Soup
(page 6) as a starter and
finish with a treat such as
Muesli Cookies (page 60).

PACKED LUNCHES

*The traditional lunchtime sandwich is always popular.
Simple to prepare, it can be as nutritious as a cooked meal.
Use a variety of breads – from crusty fresh French loaves to
wholemeal pitta breads. For something different, why not try
a soup or a salad for a super tasty snack.*

CHEESE AND BASIL SANDWICHES

For a deliciously different
sandwich, try making these
using the Onion Bread on
page 74.

4 slices bread or 2 rolls of your choice
2 tablespoons ready-made pesto
6 slices mozzarella cheese
1 tablespoon chopped fresh basil
1 tomato, sliced
freshly ground black pepper

Spread 2 bread slices or bases of rolls with
pesto. Top with mozzarella cheese, basil,
tomato and black pepper to taste, then
with remaining bread slices, or tops of
rolls. Wrap in plastic food wrap.

Makes 2 sandwiches or rolls

*Super Salad Tubes (page 46),
Cheese and Date Sandwiches (page 46),
Watercress and Brie Sandwiches (page 46),
Cheese and Basil Sandwiches*

WATERCRESS AND BRIE SANDWICHES

2 red peppers, halved and seeded
1 eggplant (aubergine), sliced
1 tablespoon vegetable oil
8 slices bread or 4 bread rolls of
your choice
$^1/_2$ bunch/125 g/4 oz watercress,
stems removed
8 slices Brie cheese
freshly ground black pepper

The sharp, peppery flavour of the watercress beautifully complements the creamiest of the Brie.

Makes 4 sandwiches or rolls

1   Place red peppers skin side up under a preheated hot grill and cook until skins blister and char. Place peppers in a paper or plastic food bag for 5-10 minutes, then remove skins.

2   Brush eggplant (aubergine) slices with oil and cook under preheated hot grill for 2-4 minutes each side or until golden.

3   Top half the bread slices or bases of rolls with watercress, red peppers, eggplant (aubergine) slices, Brie and black pepper to taste. Top with remaining bread slices or tops of rolls. Wrap in plastic food wrap.

SUPER SALAD TUBES

4 large pitta bread rounds
3 tablespoons peanut butter
2 small carrots, grated
2 raw small beetroot, grated
60 g/2 oz tasty cheese (mature
Cheddar), grated
4 lettuce leaves, shredded
$^1/_2$ small cucumber, sliced
60 g/2 oz bean sprouts

This pitta bread roll is simple to prepare and a complete meal in itself.

Spread pitta bread rounds with peanut butter. Top with carrot, beetroot, cheese, lettuce, cucumber and bean sprouts. Roll up pitta bread and wrap in greaseproof paper, then plastic food wrap.

Makes 4 tubes

CHEESE AND DATE SANDWICHES

4 slices bread of your choice
4 tablespoons cream cheese
1 tablespoon honey
8 dates, sliced
60 g/2 oz snow pea sprouts or watercress

Spread bread slices with cream cheese and drizzle with honey. Top 2 slices of bread with dates and snow pea sprouts or watercress then with remaining bread slices and wrap in plastic food wrap.

Makes 2 sandwiches

Curried Parsnip Soup

CURRIED PARSNIP SOUP

2 teaspoons vegetable oil
1 teaspoon ground coriander
1 teaspoon ground cumin
1 teaspoon ground cinnamon
$^1/_2$ teaspoon chilli powder
$^1/_2$ teaspoon ground turmeric
2 onions, chopped
750 g/1$^1/_2$ lb parsnips, chopped
5 cups/1.2 litres/2 pt vegetable stock
1 tablespoon chopped fresh coriander

1   Heat oil in a large saucepan, add ground coriander, cumin, cinnamon, chilli and turmeric and cook over a high heat, stirring constantly, for 2 minutes or until smoking.

2   Reduce heat to medium, add onions and cook, stirring constantly, for 3 minutes or until onions are soft. Add parsnips and stock, bring to the boil and simmer for 20-25 minutes or until parsnips are very soft.

3   Place soup mixture in batches in a food processor or blender and process until smooth.

4   Return soup to a clean saucepan, bring to the boil and simmer for 2 minutes or until hot. Stir in fresh coriander and pour into a warmed vacuum flask.

Serves 6

Great for a winter's lunch. Packed in a vacuum flask, this soup will still be piping hot at lunch time and is delicious eaten with a crusty bread roll.

Bowl and Plate Villeroy & Boch

GREEK POTATO SALAD

1 kg/2 lb potatoes, roughly chopped
2 teaspoons vegetable oil
2 onions, sliced
1 clove garlic, crushed
3 tablespoons white wine vinegar
185 g/6 oz black olives
1 tablespoon capers, drained
2 tablespoons chopped
flat-leaved parsley
2 tablespoons olive oil

1   Boil, steam or microwave potatoes until tender. Drain, place in a bowl and set aside to cool.

2   Heat vegetable oil in a frying pan, add onions and garlic and cook over a medium heat, stirring, for 3 minutes or until onions are soft. Add vinegar, olives, capers, parsley and olive oil to pan and mix to combine.

3   Remove pan from heat and set aside to cool. Spoon onion mixture over potatoes and toss gently to combine. Cover and refrigerate until required.

Serves 4

The most popular black olive is the Kalamata olive from Greece. It is a large purplish black olive, which lends itself to marinating.

Plate Punch Gallery

MEXICAN SALAD

1 avocado, stoned, peeled and chopped
1 tablespoon lime or lemon juice
lettuce leaves of your choice
2 tomatoes, cut into wedges
1 green pepper, chopped
315 g/10 oz canned red kidney
beans, drained
2 teaspoons chopped fresh coriander
freshly ground black pepper

1   Place avocado and lime or lemon juice
in a small bowl and toss to coat.

2   Arrange lettuce leaves, tomatoes,
green pepper, beans and avocado mixture
attractively in two lunch boxes. Sprinkle
with coriander and season to taste with
black pepper. Cover and refrigerate until
required.

Serves 2

Tossing the avocado in lime
or lemon juice helps prevent
it from discolouring.

Left: Greek Potato Salad
Above: Mexican Salad

49

OUTDOOR FEASTS

A picnic is always an enjoyable occasion. This chapter contains a variety of unusual, flavoursome pies, tarts and other foods. All the dishes are easy to transport, serve well hot or cold and are sure to be a hit.

LEEK AND APPLE ROULADE

LEEK ROULADE
60 g/2 oz butter
500 g/1 lb leeks, sliced
1 tablespoon chopped fresh thyme or
^{1}/2 teaspoon dried thyme
3 tablespoons grated Parmesan cheese
freshly ground black pepper
4 eggs, separated

APPLE FILLING
30 g/1 oz butter
^{1}/3 cup/60 g/2 oz brown sugar
1 tablespoon lemon juice
2 teaspoons ground cinnamon
3 apples, peeled and sliced

Oven temperature
190°C, 375°F, Gas 5

1 To make filling, melt butter in a large frying pan, stir in brown sugar, lemon juice and cinnamon and cook over a low heat, stirring constantly, for 2 minutes. Add apples and cook, stirring, for 1-2 minutes each side or until apples are soft and golden.

2 To make roulade, line a 26 x 32 cm/ 10^1/2 x 12^3/4 in Swiss roll tin with greased greaseproof paper. Set aside. Melt butter in a saucepan, add leeks and cook over a medium heat, stirring, for 6 minutes or until leeks are soft. Remove pan from heat and set aside to cool slightly.

3 Place leek mixture in a food processor or blender and process until finely chopped. Place leek mixture, thyme, Parmesan cheese, black pepper to taste and egg yolks in a bowl and mix to combine.

4 Place egg whites in a separate bowl and beat until stiff peaks form. Fold egg white mixture into leek mixture. Carefully spoon roulade mixture into prepared tin and bake for 10-15 minutes or until cooked.

5 Turn roulade onto a damp teatowel and peel away paper. Spread filling over roulade, roll up tightly and wrap in a clean teatowel to transport to your picnic.

Serves 6

To serve, cut the roulade into slices and accompany with a salad of mixed lettuces and fresh herbs.

Leek and Apple Roulade, Asparagus and Camembert Pie (page 52)

ASPARAGUS AND CAMEMBERT PIE

Oven temperature
180°C, 350°F, Gas 4

Delicious hot, warm or cold, all this pie needs to make a complete meal is a green salad and crusty bread. If fresh asparagus is unavailable this pie is also delicious made with well-drained canned asparagus.

4 sheets filo pastry
60 g/2 oz butter, melted
100 g/3¹/₂ oz flaked almonds
250 g/8 oz asparagus spears, trimmed
60 g/2 oz sun-dried tomatoes, sliced
125 g/4 oz button mushrooms, sliced
125 g/4 oz Camembert cheese, sliced
2 eggs, lightly beaten
¹/₃ cup/90 mL/3 fl oz cream (double)
or milk

1   Brush each sheet of filo pastry with melted butter and sprinkle with almonds. Layer pastry and place in a greased 18 x 28 cm/7 x 11 in shallow cake tin. Trim overhanging edges.

2   Top pastry with asparagus, sun-dried tomatoes, mushrooms and Camembert cheese.

3   Place eggs and cream or milk in a bowl and whisk to combine. Carefully pour egg mixture over vegetable mixture and bake for 35-40 minutes or until pie is firm and top golden.

Serves 6

TOMATO AND OLIVE TART

Oven temperature
180°C, 350°F, Gas 4

This savoury tart is delicious served warm or cold with a salad, such as Chickpea and Pepper Salad (page 16).

250 g/8 oz prepared puff pastry
1 egg, lightly beaten

TOMATO AND OLIVE TOPPING
2 teaspoons vegetable oil
1 onion, chopped
5 tomatoes, peeled, seeded and chopped
2 tablespoons tomato paste (purée)
¹/₃ cup/90 mL/3 fl oz red wine
2 teaspoons sugar
3 tablespoons shredded fresh basil leaves
2 red peppers, roasted and skins removed
185 g/6 oz pitted black olives

1   Roll out pastry to 5 mm/¹/₄ in thick. Cut pastry into a 20 x 30 cm/8 x 12 in rectangle and place on a greased baking tray. Brush edges with egg. Cut 2 cm/³/₄ in wide strips from remaining pastry and place around the edge of rectangle to make a border.

2   To make topping, heat oil in a frying pan, add onion and cook over a medium heat, stirring, for 3 minutes or until onion is soft. Add tomatoes, tomato paste (purée), wine, sugar and basil and cook over a low heat, stirring constantly, for 20 minutes or until mixture reduces and thickens. Remove pan from heat and set aside to cool slightly.

3   Spread tomato mixture over pastry. Cut red peppers into strips and arrange in a diamond pattern over tomato mixture. Place olives in centre of diamonds and bake for 30 minutes or until pastry is puffed and golden.

Serves 6

Potato Tart, Tomato and Olive Tart

POTATO TART

200 g/6^1/$_2$ oz prepared shortcrust pastry

POTATO FILLING
500 g/1 lb potatoes
2 teaspoons vegetable oil
2 leeks, sliced
125 g/4 oz Camembert cheese, sliced
300 g/9^1/$_2$ oz sour cream
^{1}/$_2$ teaspoon ground nutmeg
freshly ground black pepper

1 Roll out pastry to 5 mm/^{1}/$_4$ in thick and use to line a greased 23 cm/9 in flan tin. Prick base and sides of pastry with a fork, line with nonstick baking paper and fill with uncooked rice. Bake for 10 minutes or until lightly browned, then remove rice and paper and set aside to cool.

2 Boil or microwave potatoes until soft. Drain, slice and set aside to cool.

3 Heat oil in small frying pan, add leeks and cook over a medium heat, stirring constantly, for 5 minutes or until golden. Set aside to cool.

4 Spread leeks over base of pastry case, top with potato slices and Camembert cheese.

5 Place sour cream, nutmeg and black pepper to taste in a bowl and mix to combine. Spoon sour cream mixture over filling and bake for 10-15 minutes or until top is golden.

Serves 6

Oven temperature
180°C, 350°F, Gas 4

Warm or cold, this tart makes a perfect picnic lunch and is delicious accompanied by a mixed vegetable salad.

HUMMUS AND VEGETABLE TERRINE

1 bunch/500 g/1 lb spinach,
stalks removed
4 zucchini (courgettes), sliced
4 carrots, sliced
2 avocados, stoned, peeled and mashed
3 tablespoons mayonnaise
1 tablespoon lemon juice
1 cup/220 g/7 oz rice, cooked
3 red peppers, halved, roasted and skins
removed, chopped
200 g/6^{1}/2 oz hummus

5 Pack half the rice into spinach-lined loaf tin, pressing down well with the back of a spoon. Top with half the red peppers, zucchini (courgettes), carrots and hummus. Spread with avocado mixture, then top with remaining rice, red peppers, zucchini (courgettes), carrots and, lastly, hummus.

1 Line an 11 x 21 cm/4^{1}/2 x 8^{1}/2 in loaf tin with plastic food wrap. Set aside.

2 Boil, steam or microwave spinach leaves until just wilted. Drain well. Line prepared loaf tin with overlapping spinach leaves. Allow leaves to overhang the sides of the tin.

3 Boil, steam or microwave zucchini (courgettes) and carrots, separately, until just tender. Drain and set aside.

4 Place avocados, mayonnaise and lemon juice in a bowl and mix to combine. Set aside.

6 Fold overhanging spinach leaves over filling. Place a heavy weight on terrine and refrigerate for at least 4 hours before serving. To serve, unmould and cut into slices.

Serves 6-8

Hummus is a popular Middle Eastern dip made from a purée of cooked chickpeas and tahini (sesame paste). Hummus is available from delicatessens and some supermarkets, or you can make your own. To make hummus, place 185 g/6 oz cooked or canned chickpeas, 2 cloves garlic, crushed, 1 tablespoon lemon juice and 90 g/3 oz tahini paste in a food processor or blender and process to make a smooth paste.

Plate: Robyn Donoghue

PICNIC BHAJAS

Bhajas are delicious served hot, warm or cold. For a tasty treat place bhajas on flatbread such as pitta bread or naan, top with natural yogurt and mango chutney, roll up and enjoy.
Besan flour is flour made from chickpeas and is available from Asian food stores.

2 eggs, lightly beaten
$^1/4$ cup/60 mL/2 fl oz milk
45 g/1$^1/2$ oz red lentils, washed
1 red onion, chopped
1 carrot, grated
75 g/2$^1/2$ oz canned sweet corn kernels, drained
1 potato, grated
155 g/5 oz besan flour
$^1/4$ teaspoon baking powder
1 teaspoon ground cumin
1 teaspoon ground nutmeg
1 teaspoon ground turmeric
2 tablespoons chopped fresh coriander
vegetable oil for deep-frying

1   Place eggs, milk, lentils, onion, carrot, sweet corn, potato, flour, baking powder, cumin, nutmeg, turmeric and coriander in a bowl and mix well to combine.

2   Heat oil in a large saucepan until a cube of bread dropped in browns in 50 seconds. Drop heaped tablespoons of mixture into oil and deep-fry for 1-2 minutes or until golden. Drain on absorbent kitchen paper.

Serves 4-6

MINIATURE BERRY PIES

200 g/6¹/2 oz prepared sweet
shortcrust pastry
1 egg, lightly beaten
2 tablespoons sugar

BERRY FILLING
250 g/8 oz fresh or frozen mixed berries
¹/3 cup/90 mL/3 fl oz orange juice
1 tablespoon sugar
2 teaspoons arrowroot blended with
1 tablespoon water

1   To make filling, place berries, orange juice, sugar and arrowroot mixture in a small saucepan and cook over a low heat, stirring constantly, until mixture thickens. Remove pan from heat and set aside to cool completely.

2   Roll out pastry to 3 mm/¹/8 in thick. Using a 7.5 cm/3 in cutter, cut twelve pastry rounds and place in lightly greased patty cake tins.

3   Using a 5 cm/2 in cutter, cut twelve rounds from remaining pastry and set aside.

4   Place a spoonful of cold filling in each pastry base, brush edges with egg and top with remaining pastry rounds, press edges together to seal. Brush tops with egg, sprinkle with sugar and bake for 25-30 minutes or until pastry is golden.

Left: Picnic Bhajas
Above: Miniature Berry Pies   ***Makes 12***

Oven temperature
180°C, 350°F, Gas 4

Use strawberries, raspberries or blueberries. The combination of crisp pastry and tangy berries makes these little pies delicious. Serve them with whipped cream with a touch of spice added.

SPECIAL TREATS

*This chapter contains a selection of great-tasting
cakes and cookies, muffins and scones that are almost too
good to be true. These home-baked treats make perfect
between-meal snacks or delicious desserts.*

COCONUT SCONES

Oven temperature
220°C, 425°F, Gas 7

2 cups/250 g/8 oz self-raising flour
1 teaspoon baking powder
2 teaspoons sugar
2 tablespoons desiccated coconut
45 g/1¹/₂ oz butter
1 egg, lightly beaten
³/₄-1 cup/185-250 mL/6-8 fl oz
coconut milk
milk

1   Sift together flour and baking powder
into a bowl. Stir in sugar and coconut.

2   Rub in butter with fingertips until
mixture resembles coarse breadcrumbs.
Mix in egg and enough coconut milk to
form a soft dough.

3   Turn dough onto a lightly floured
surface and knead briefly. Press dough out
to 2 cm/³/₄ in thick and, using a 5 cm/2 in
cutter, cut out twelve rounds and place
close together on a greased baking tray.

4   Brush tops of scones with a little milk
and bake for 12-15 minutes or until
golden.

Makes 12

These scones are delicious
served warm with whipped
cream or natural yogurt and
strawberry jam.

*Carob Nut Clusters (page 60),
Double-Choc Muffins (page 60)*

DOUBLE-CHOC MUFFINS

1³/4 cups/220 g/7 oz self-raising flour
¹/2 teaspoon baking powder
¹/4 cup/30 g/1 oz cocoa powder
¹/2 cup/90 g/3 oz brown sugar
1 egg, lightly beaten
³/4 cup/185 mL/6 fl oz milk
¹/4 cup/60 mL/2 fl oz vegetable oil
125 g/4 oz chocolate, chopped

1   Sift together flour, baking powder and cocoa powder into a bowl. Stir in sugar, egg, milk, oil and chocolate, and mix to combine.

2   Spoon mixture into six lightly greased large muffin tins and bake for 20-25 minutes or until cooked when tested with a skewer.

Makes 6

CAROB NUT CLUSTERS

Carob is the dried ground seeds of the carob tree. It comes in a powdered form similar to cocoa powder and in a block form similar to chocolate. This recipe uses the block form. Carob is caffeine-free but, unfortunately, it is no lower in kilojoules (calories) than chocolate.

250 g/8 oz carob
45 g/1¹/2 oz butter
¹/3 cup/90 mL/3 fl oz cream (double)
100 g/3¹/2 oz roasted unsalted mixed nuts
4 tablespoons shredded coconut, toasted

Makes about 30

1   Place carob and butter in a small saucepan and cook over a low heat, stirring constantly, until melted and smooth. Stir in cream, nuts and coconut and cook, stirring, for 1 minute longer.

2   Spoon tablespoons of mixture onto a foil-lined tray or into paper patty cases and refrigerate for 1 hour or until set.

MUESLI COOKIES

1 cup/125 g/4 oz self-raising flour
1 cup/155 g/5 oz wholemeal self-raising flour
3 tablespoons sugar
90 g/3 oz butter
³/4 cup/90 g/3 oz toasted muesli
1 tablespoon finely grated orange rind
1 egg, lightly beaten
¹/3 cup/90 mL/3 fl oz milk

Pop some of these cookies into a lunch box for a special lunchtime treat. They taste great and are good for you.

1   Place self-raising flour, wholemeal self-raising flour and sugar in a bowl and mix to combine. Rub in butter with fingertips until mixture resembles fine breadcrumbs.

2   Stir in muesli, orange rind, egg and milk and mix to form a soft dough.

3   Drop tablespoons of mixture onto greased baking trays and bake for 12-15 minutes or until golden brown. Stand on trays for 3 minutes before transferring to wire racks to cool.

Makes 30

Muesli Cookies, Lavender Cookies

LAVENDER COOKIES

125 g/4 oz butter, chopped
³/4 cup/125 g/4 oz icing sugar
1¹/2 cups/185 g/6 oz flour
¹/3 cup/90 g/3 oz sour cream
3 teaspoons lemon juice
2 teaspoons dried lavender flowers

1 Place butter, icing sugar, flour, sour cream, lemon juice and lavender flowers in a food processor or blender and process until smooth.

2 Drop spoonfuls of mixture onto greased baking trays and bake for 10-12 minutes or until lightly browned. Cool on trays.

Makes 40

Oven temperature
180°C, 350°F, Gas 4

Dried lavender flowers are available from health food shops. They add a deliciously different taste to these special cookies.

CARROT AND ALMOND CAKE

Oven temperature
180°C, 350°F, Gas 4

4 eggs, separated
1 cup/250 g/8 oz sugar
2 tablespoons finely grated orange rind
250 g/8 oz finely grated carrots
250 g/8 oz blanched almonds,
finely chopped
2 tablespoons self-raising flour, sifted
2 tablespoons pine nuts

1   Place egg yolks, sugar and orange rind in a large bowl and beat with an electric mixer for 3 minutes or until thick and fluffy. Add carrots, almonds and flour and mix gently to combine.

2   Place egg whites in a separate bowl and beat until stiff peaks form. Fold egg white mixture into carrot mixture.

3   Pour batter into a greased and lined 20 cm/8 in round cake tin. Sprinkle with pine nuts and bake for 45 minutes or until cooked when tested with a skewer. Stand cake in tin for 5 minutes before turning onto a wire rack to cool.

Makes a 20 cm/8 in round cake

For a special treat this cake is delicious served warm with vanilla yogurt.

COUNTRY POLENTA CAKE

Oven temperature
150°C, 300°F, Gas 2

60 g/2 oz sultanas
2 tablespoons brandy
220 g/7 oz ricotta cheese
2 cups/500 mL/16 fl oz water
1 cup/220 g/7 oz caster sugar
$1^{1}/4$ cups/220 g/7 oz corn meal (polenta)
2 cups/250 g/8 oz self-raising flour
125 g/4 oz butter, melted
1 teaspoon ground cinnamon
3 tablespoons chopped hazelnuts

1   Place sultanas in a small bowl, pour over brandy and set aside to macerate for 20 minutes.

2   Place ricotta cheese and water in a bowl and whisk to combine. Stir in sugar.

3   Gradually whisk in corn meal (polenta) and flour and continue to whisk until well combined. Stir in sultana mixture, butter, cinnamon and hazelnuts.

4   Pour batter into a greased 25 cm/10 in springform tin and bake for $1^{3}/4$ hours or until cooked when tested with a skewer. Stand in tin for 5 minutes before turning out. Serve warm.

Makes a 25 cm/10 in round cake

Corn meal (polenta) gives this cake an interesting texture. It makes a tasty between-meal snack or a delicious finish to a casual meal.

Country Polenta Cake, Carrot and Almond Cake,
Coconut Scones (page 58)

DREAMY DESSERTS

*From light and refreshing fruit dishes to more hearty
baked puddings, the desserts in this chapter are a perfect ending
to a nourishing and delicious meal.*

BAKED APPLE CHEESECAKE

Oven temperature
190°C, 375°F, Gas 5

200 g/6^1/$_2$ oz prepared shortcrust pastry
30 g/1 oz butter
2 apples, cored, peeled and sliced

RICOTTA FILLING
750 g/1^1/$_2$ lb ricotta cheese
4 eggs, separated
^{1}/$_2$ cup/170 g/5^1/$_2$ oz honey
1 tablespoon finely grated orange rind
3 tablespoons orange juice

1   Roll out pastry to 3 mm/^{1}/$_8$ in thick
and use to line a deep 23 cm/9 in flan tin
with a removable base. Prick base and
sides of pastry with a fork, line with
nonstick baking paper and fill with
uncooked rice. Bake for 10 minutes, then
remove rice and paper and bake for 5-8
minutes longer or until lightly browned.

2   Melt butter in a frying pan, add apple
slices and cook over a medium heat,
stirring occasionally, until golden. Set
aside to cool. Arrange apples evenly over
base of pastry case.

3   To make filling, place ricotta cheese,
egg yolks, honey, orange rind and orange
juice in a food processor or blender and
process until smooth.

4   Place egg whites in a separate bowl
and beat until stiff peaks form. Fold egg
white mixture into ricotta mixture.
Carefully pour filling over apples.

5   Reduce oven temperature to 180°C/
350°F/Gas 4 and bake for 1^1/$_4$ hours or
until firm. Set aside to cool, then
refrigerate overnight.

Serves 8

This cheesecake is also
delicious made with other
fruits, such as pears, apricots
or peaches.

Baked Apple Cheesecake

BAKED MANDARIN SABAYON

Oven temperature
180°C, 350°F, Gas 4

**4 mandarins, peeled, broken
into segments and white pith removed
2 tablespoons icing sugar**

BRANDY SABAYON
**4 egg yolks
$^1/_4$ cup/60 mL/2 fl oz brandy
$^1/_4$ cup/60 g/2 oz caster sugar**

The sweet sabayon sauce is a perfect accompaniment to the tangy taste of the mandarin.

1   Place mandarin segments, overlapping and in a spiral pattern, on four ovenproof serving plates. Set aside.

2   To make sabayon, place egg yolks, brandy and caster sugar in a heatproof bowl set over a saucepan of simmering water and beat for 5 minutes or until thick and creamy.

3   Pour sabayon over mandarins, sprinkle with icing sugar and bake for 3-4 minutes or until lightly browned. Serve immediately.

Serves 4

Plate Villeroy & Boch

Plate Villeroy & Boch

SUGAR ROAST FRUITS

**2 peaches, sliced
2 pears, cored and sliced
2 apples, cored and sliced
1 mango, sliced
$^1/_2$ cup/125 g/4 oz sugar**

PASSION FRUIT COULIS
**6 passion fruit or 6 tablespoons
passion fruit pulp**

1 Place peaches, pears, apples and mango on a baking tray. Sprinkle with sugar and cook under a preheated medium grill for 5 minutes or until sugar is golden.

2 To make coulis, place passion fruit pulp in a food processor or blender and process to finely chop.

3 Arrange fruit on serving plates, and serve with coulis.

*Left: Baked Mandarin Sabayon
Above: Sugar Roast Fruits*

Serves 4

Serve this deliciously light dessert after a hearty main meal such as a pasta bake or risotto.

CARAMELISED RICE PUDDINGS

1 cup/250 g/8 oz sugar
$^1/_2$ cup/125 mL/4 fl oz water
1 cup/220 g/7 oz short grain rice
3$^1/_2$ cups/875 mL/1$^1/_2$ pt milk
1 teaspoon vanilla essence
4 egg yolks
$^1/_2$ cup/100 g/3$^1/_2$ oz caster sugar
30 g/1 oz unsalted butter

1   Place sugar and water in a small saucepan and cook over a low heat, stirring constantly, until sugar dissolves. Bring to the boil and cook, without stirring, until lightly golden.

2   Pour toffee into four lightly greased 1 cup/250 mL/8 fl oz capacity ramekins or moulds. Set aside to harden.

5   Divide rice mixture between toffee-lined ramekins or moulds, cover and refrigerate overnight.

3   Place rice, milk and vanilla essence in a saucepan and cook over a medium heat, stirring, for 15 minutes or until rice is soft. Remove from heat and set aside to cool slightly.

4   Place egg yolks and sugar in a bowl and whisk to combine. Stir egg mixture and butter into rice mixture and mix well to combine.

6   To serve, dip the base of ramekins or moulds in hot water, then invert onto serving plates.

Serves 4

This luscious tasting version of an old favourite is sure to appeal, even to those who think they don't like rice pudding. Try it served with poached or fresh fruit.

Plate Villeroy & Boch

Above: Quinces with Honey Cream
Right: French Bread Pudding

QUINCES WITH HONEY CREAM

6 cups/1.5 litres/2^1/$_2$ pt water
1^1/$_2$ cups/375 g/12 oz sugar
4 strips lemon rind
6 quinces, peeled and quartered
^{3}/4 cup/185 mL/6 fl oz cream
(double), whipped
3 tablespoons honey

1 Place water and sugar in a large saucepan and cook over a low heat, stirring constantly, until sugar dissolves.

2 Add lemon rind and quinces to syrup, bring to the boil and simmer for 40 minutes or until quinces are tender and change colour.

3 To serve, place quinces on serving plates, spoon over a little of the cooking liquid, accompany with cream and drizzle with honey.

Serves 6

If quinces are unavailable, this recipe is also good made with apples or pears. The cooking time will not be as long.

FRENCH BREAD PUDDING

1 loaf brioche, sliced
6 eggs, lightly beaten
1¹/₂ cups/375 mL/12 fl oz milk
1 teaspoon vanilla essence
1 teaspoon ground nutmeg

FRUIT FILLING
125 g/4 oz dried figs, chopped
125 g/4 oz dried dates, pitted
and chopped
¹/₂ cup/125 mL/4 fl oz orange juice
¹/₃ cup/90 mL/3 fl oz brandy
1 cinnamon stick

1 To make filling, place figs, dates, orange juice, brandy and cinnamon stick in a saucepan and cook over a low heat, stirring, for 15-20 minutes or until fruit is soft and mixture thick. Remove cinnamon stick.

2 To assemble pudding, place one-third of the brioche slices in the base of a greased 11 x 21 cm/4¹/₂ x 8¹/₂ in loaf tin. Top with half the filling. Repeat layers, ending with a layer of brioche.

3 Place eggs, milk, vanilla essence and nutmeg in a bowl and whisk to combine. Carefully pour egg mixture over brioche and fruit and set aside to stand for 5 minutes. Place tin in a baking dish with enough boiling water to come halfway up the sides of the tin and bake for 45 minutes or until firm. Stand pudding in tin for 10 minutes before turning out and serving.

Serves 6-8

Oven temperature
160°C, 325°F, Gas 3

This tempting dessert is best eaten cut into slices and served with cream shortly after it is turned out of the tin.

BREADS AND SPREADS

Spreads are the vegetarian alternative to pâté. Serve them with fresh raw vegetables for dipping, or spread them on the homemade breads in this chapter for a sandwich taste sensation. Team the breads with dishes from earlier chapters and you have a well-rounded, wholesome and appetising meal.

VEGETABLE HERB BREAD

Oven temperature
180°C, 350°F, Gas 4

2 teaspoons vegetable oil
2 onions, finely chopped
200 g/6^{1}/$_{2}$ oz button mushrooms, sliced
60 g/2 oz sun-dried tomatoes, chopped
375 g/12 oz packet scone mix
3 tablespoons vegetable oil
3 eggs, lightly beaten
3 tablespoons grated Parmesan cheese
1 tablespoon chopped fresh thyme or
^{1}/$_{2}$ teaspoon dried thyme
2 tablespoons chopped fresh parsley

1   Heat oil in a frying pan, add onions and cook over a medium heat, stirring, for 3 minutes or until onions are soft. Add mushrooms and sun-dried tomatoes and cook for 2 minutes longer. Remove pan from heat and set aside to cool.

2   Place scone mix in a bowl. Make a well in the centre and stir in oil, eggs, Parmesan cheese, thyme, parsley and vegetable mixture and mix well to form a rough batter.

3   Pour batter into a well-greased 11 x 21 cm/4^{1}/$_{2}$ x 8^{1}/$_{2}$ in loaf tin and bake for 50 minutes or until cooked when tested with a skewer.

Makes an 11 x 21 cm/4^{1}/$_{2}$ x 8^{1}/$_{2}$ in loaf

Eaten warm, Vegetable Herb Bread is delicious on its own, or served with salad, or with a bowl of steaming hot soup.

Vegetable Herb Bread, Onion Bread (page 74), Cheese and Basil Bread (page 75)

ONION BREAD

Oven temperature
220°C, 425°F, Gas 7

15 g/^{1}/$_2$ oz fresh yeast
155 mL/5 fl oz warm water
1^3/$_4$ cups/220 g/7 oz flour
1 tablespoon olive oil
125 g/4 oz pitted black olives
1 tablespoon chopped fresh rosemary or
^{1}/$_2$ teaspoon dried rosemary
freshly ground black pepper

ONION TOPPING
1 tablespoon vegetable oil
15 g/^{1}/$_2$ oz butter
5 onions, sliced
2 cloves garlic, crushed
2 tablespoons vinegar

1   To make topping, heat vegetable oil and butter in a large frying pan, add onions and garlic and cook over a low heat, stirring occasionally, for 20 minutes or until onions are soft and golden. Add vinegar and cook, stirring, for 1 minute longer. Remove pan from heat and set aside to cool.

2   Dissolve yeast in half the water in a small bowl and set aside in a warm place until frothy.

3   Sift flour in a large bowl. Make a well in the centre of the flour, add yeast mixture, remaining water and olive oil and mix to form a dough.

4   Turn dough onto a lightly floured surface and knead for 10 minutes or until dough is smooth and elastic.

5   Place dough in an oiled bowl, cover with a clean teatowel and stand in a warm, draught-free place for 10 minutes or until doubled in size. Punch down, turn onto a lightly floured surface and knead again for 1 minute.

6   Press dough into a greased 26 x 32 cm/ 10^1/$_2$ x 12^3/$_4$ in Swiss roll tin. Top with onion mixture, olives, rosemary and black pepper to taste. Bake for 25 minutes or until dough rises and bread is golden. Serve hot or cold, cut into wedges.

Serves 6

This pizza-like bread makes a delicious lunch when served with Asparagus and Cheese Tart (page 35).

YOGURT HERB SPREAD

^{1}/$_2$ cup/100 g/3^1/$_2$ oz natural yogurt
1 tablespoon chopped fresh basil
1 tablespoon snipped fresh chives
1 tablespoon chopped fresh parsley
2 teaspoons Worcestershire sauce
freshly ground black pepper

Place yogurt, basil, chives, parsley, Worcestershire sauce and black pepper to taste in a bowl and mix to combine. Cover and refrigerate until required.

Makes ^{3}/$_4$ cup/185 g/6 oz

Serve this spread with crusty fresh bread rolls for lunch.

Fruit and Ricotta Spread (page 76),
Blue Cheese Spread (page 76),
Mexican Spread (page 76), Yogurt Herb Spread

CHEESE AND BASIL BREAD

1¹/₂ cups/185 g/6 oz self-raising flour
³/₄ cup/125 g/4 oz wholemeal
self-raising flour
¹/₂ teaspoon bicarbonate of soda
90 g/3 oz tasty cheese (mature
Cheddar), grated
4 tablespoons chopped fresh basil
155 mL/5 fl oz buttermilk or milk
2-3 tablespoons water
extra tasty cheese (mature
Cheddar), grated

Makes an 11 x 21 cm/4¹/₂ x 8¹/₂ in loaf

1   Sift together self-raising flour, wholemeal self-raising flour and bicarbonate of soda into a bowl. Return husks to bowl, add cheese and basil and mix to combine.

2   Make a well in the centre of the flour mixture and mix in milk and enough water to form a soft dough. Turn dough onto a lightly floured surface and knead briefly.

3   Shape dough and place in a greased 11 x 21 cm/4¹/₂ x 8¹/₂ in loaf tin, sprinkle with extra cheese and bake 1 hour or until cooked when tested with a skewer.

Oven temperature
190°C, 375°F, Gas 5

Cheese and Basil Bread is the perfect accompaniment to a bowl of hot Ripe Red Tomato Soup (page 6).

Blue Cheese Spread

125 g/4 oz creamy blue cheese
¹/4 cup/60 g/2 oz sour cream or yogurt
2 tablespoons snipped fresh chives
freshly ground black pepper

Place blue cheese and sour cream or yogurt in a bowl and mix to combine. Stir in chives and black pepper to taste. Cover and refrigerate until required.

Makes ³/4 cup/185 g/6 oz

Use creamy Castello or Stilton cheese. This spread tastes great on baked potatoes.

Mexican Spread

125 g/4 oz cream cheese, softened
3 tablespoons tomato paste (purée)
¹/2 green pepper, finely chopped
¹/2 teaspoon ground cumin
1 teaspoon chilli powder

Place cream cheese, tomato paste (purée), green pepper, cumin and chilli powder in a bowl and mix to combine. Cover and refrigerate until required.

Makes ³/4 cup/185 g/6 oz

Serve this spread with wholemeal toast slices or as a dip accompanied by freshly cut crudités.

Fruit and Ricotta Spread

125 g/4 oz ricotta cheese, drained
6 dried apricots, chopped
2 tablespoons currants
3 tablespoons chopped dried apple
4 dried dates, chopped
2 teaspoons finely grated lemon rind
1 tablespoon lemon juice
1 tablespoon honey

Place ricotta cheese, apricots, currants, apple, dates, lemon rind, lemon juice and honey in a bowl and mix to combine. Cover and refrigerate until required.

Makes 1 cup/250 g/8 oz

Delicious spread on crackers or pieces of celery for a party starter.

Menu Ideas

For many people – particularly those new to vegetarianism – serving a vegetarian meal is a problem, as the foods that combine to make a nutritiously balanced meal do not always go together well on a plate. One way around this is to serve several courses. As you will see, some of these menus have been designed to be served in this way.

SUMMER LUNCH PARTY FOR SIX

Serve this tempting summer luncheon buffet-style, and outdoors if the weather permits.

Mediterranean Rocket Salad
(page 10)
Lentil and Mushroom Salad
(page 14)
Black-eyed Bean Salad
(page 16)

Ricotta and Basil Lasagne
(page 32)

Onion Bread
(page 74)
Yogurt Herb Spread
(page 74)

Country Polenta Cake
(page 62)
Vanilla Yogurt

SPEEDY FAMILY MEAL FOR FOUR

Goat's Cheese and Polenta Pizza
(page 18)
Tossed Green Salad

Double-Choc Muffins
(page 60)

HEARTY WINTER DINNER
FOR SIX
Cream of Lentil Soup
(page 6)
Wholegrain Rolls

Watercress and Orange Salad
(page 12)
Pasta with Chickpeas and Feta
(page 24)

Caramelised Rice Puddings
(page 68)
(Make up $1^1/_2$ recipe quantity)

FAMILY DINNER FOR FOUR
Ripe Red Tomato Soup
(page 6)
Vegetable Herb Bread
(page 72)

Mushroom Risotto
(page 40)
Tossed Green Salad

Carrot and Almond Cake
(page 62)
Vanilla Yogurt

DINNER PARTY FOR EIGHT
Snow Pea Soup and Cheese Toasts
(page 7)
Italian Salad
(page 17)

Okra and Bean Stew
(page 30)
Boiled or Steamed Brown Rice

Baked Mandarin Sabayon
(page 66)

INDEX

Apple Cheesecake 64
Asparagus
    and Camembert Pie 52
    and Cheese Tart 35
Aubergine *see* Eggplant
Avocado Salsa 39
Baked Polenta Sandwiches 36
Beans
    Mexican Salad 49
    and Okra Stew 30
    Salad 16
Berry Pies 57
Bhajas, Picnic 56
Black-eyed Bean Salad 16
Blue Cheese
    and Celery Soup 4
    Spread 76
Bread
    Cheese and Basil 75
    Onion 74
    Vegetable Herb 72
Bread Pudding, French 71
Brie and Watercress Sandwiches 46
Buckwheat Noodles 21
Cake
    Carrot and Almond 62
    Country Polenta 62
Camembert and Asparagus Pie 52
Caramelised Rice Puddings 68
Carob Nut Clusters 60
Carrot
    and Almond Cake 62
    and Orange Soup 8
Celery and Blue Cheese Soup 4
Cheese
    see also Blue Cheese; Feta Cheese;
        Goat's Cheese; Ricotta
    Asparagus and Camembert Pie 52
    and Asparagus Tart 35
    and Basil Bread 75
    and Basil Sandwiches 44
    and Date Sandwiches 46
    Toasts 7
    Watercress and Brie Sandwiches 46
    Watercress and Stilton Pizza 20
Cheesecake, Apple 64
Chickpeas
    and Feta Pasta 24
    Hummus and Vegetable Terrine 54
    and Pepper Salad 16

Chilli
    Pasta Bake 32
    Sauce 32
    Sesame Dressing 13
Chocolate Muffins 60
Chutney, Rhubarb 42
Coconut Scones 58
Cookies
    Lavender 61
    Muesli 60
Corn Meal *see* Polenta
Coulis, Passion Fruit 67
Country Polenta Cake 62
Cream Cheese and Date
    Sandwiches 46
Cream of Lentil Soup 6
Curry
    Parsnip Soup 47
    Vegetable, with Chutney 42
Double-Choc Muffins 60
Dressing
    Chilli Sesame 13
    Honey 14
    Orange 12
    Pesto 17
    Pine Nut 16
Eggplant Kebabs 26
Endive and Goat's Cheese Salad 14
Feta Cheese
    and Chickpeas Pasta 24
    and Herb Fritters 39
French Bread Pudding 71
Frittata, Mushroom 28
Fritters, Cheese and Herb 39
Fruit
    and Ricotta Spread 76
    Sugar Roast 67
Gnocchi, Sun-dried Tomato 38
Goat's Cheese
    and Endive Salad 14
    and Polenta Pizza 18
Greek Potato Salad 48
Green Omelette 22
Herb
    Bread 72
    and Potato Tortilla 23
    Yogurt Spread 74
Honey Dressing 14
Hummus and Vegetable Terrine 54
Italian Potato Bake 34
Italian Salad 17
Kebabs, Eggplant 26
Kidney Beans
    Mexican Salad 49
    and Okra Stew 30
Lasagne, Ricotta and Basil 32

Lavender Cookies 61
Leek and Apple Roulade 50
Lentils
    Cream Soup 6
    and Mushroom Salad 14
    Picnic Bhajas 56
Mandarin Sabayon 66
Mediterranean Rocket Salad 10
Mexican Salad 49
Mexican Spread 76
Mozzarella Cheese and Basil
    Sandwiches 44
Muesli Cookies 60
Muffins, Chocolate 60
Mushroom
    Frittata 28
    and Lentil Salad 14
    Risotto 40
Nashi and Nut Salad 13
Noodles
    Soup, Oriental 8
    Spicy Buckwheat 21
Okra and Bean Stew 30
Olive
    Sauce 38
    and Tomato Tart 52
Omelette
    Green 22
    Herb and Potato Tortilla 23
    Mushroom Frittata 28
Onion Bread 74
Orange Dressing 12
Oriental Noodle Soup 8
Pancakes, Spinach 22
Parsnip Soup, Curried 47
Passion Fruit Coulis 67
Pasta
    with Chickpeas and Feta 24
    Chilli Bake 32
    with Fresh Thyme 24
    Ricotta and Basil Lasagne 32
    Sun-dried Tomato Gnocchi 38
    Tagliarini with Pistachios 33
Pepper and Chickpea Salad 16
Pesto Dressing 17
Picnic Bhajas 56
Pies, Dessert: Berry 57
Pies, Savoury: Asparagus and
    Camembert 52
Pine Nut Dressing 16
Pitta Bread Super Salad Tubes 46
Pizza
    Goat's Cheese and Polenta 18
    Watercress and Stilton 20
Polenta
    Cake 62

and Goat's Cheese Pizza 18
Sandwiches 36
Potato
    Bake, Italian 34
    and Herb Tortilla 23
    Salad, Greek 48
    Tart 53
Quinces with Honey Cream 70
Rhubarb Chutney 42
Rice
    see also Risotto
    Caramelised Puddings 68
    Spinach Parcels 27
Ricotta
    and Basil Lasagne 32
    and Fruit Spread 76
Ripe Red Tomato Soup 6
Risotto
    Mushroom 40
    Tomato 40
Rocket Salad 10
Sabayon, Mandarin 66
Saffron Cream with Vegetables 43
Salad
    Black-eyed Bean 16
    Chickpea and Pepper 16
    Goat's Cheese and Endive 14
    Greek Potato 48
    Italian 17
    Lentil and Mushroom 14
    Mexican 49
    Nashi and Nut 13

    Rocket 10
    Watercress and Orange 12
Sandwiches
    Baked Polenta 36
    Cheese and Basil 44
    Cheese and Date 46
    Watercress and Brie 46
Sauce, Savoury
    Avocado Salsa 39
    Chilli 32
    Olive 38
    Saffron Cream 43
    Tomato 32
    Yogurt 26
Sauce, Sweet: Passion Fruit Coulis 67
Scones, Coconut 58
Smoked Cheese and Asparagus Tart 35
Snow Pea Soup 7
Sorrel Omelette 22
Soup
    Carrot and Orange 8
    Celery and Blue Cheese 4
    Cream of Lentil 6
    Curried Parsnip 47
    Oriental Noodle 8
    Ripe Red Tomato 6
    Snow Pea 7
Spicy Buckwheat Noodles 21
Spinach
    Pancakes 22
    Rice Parcels 27
Spread

Blue Cheese 76
Fruit and Ricotta 76
Mexican 76
Yogurt Herb 74
Stilton and Watercress Pizza 20
Stir-Fry, Vegetable 29
Sugar Roast Fruits 67
Sun-dried Tomato Gnocchi 38
Super Salad Tubes 46
Tagliarini with Pistachios 33
Tart
    Asparagus and Cheese 35
    Potato 53
    Tomato and Olive 52
Terrine, Hummus and Vegetable 54
Thyme Pasta 24
Toasts, Cheese 7
Tomato
    and Olive Tart 52
    Risotto 40
    Sauce 32
    Soup 6
Tomatoes, Sun-dried, Gnocchi 38
Tortilla, Herb and Potato 23
Watercress
    and Brie Sandwiches 46
    and Orange Salad 12
    and Stilton Pizzas 20
Yogurt
    Herb Spread 74
    Sauce 26